Gabby
Invents the
Perfect Hair Bow

Words by Erica Swallow
Pictures by Li Zeng

Entrepreneur
Kid

For little ladies and sweet peas everywhere who dare to dream big.
— E.S.

For Erica, Dan, Mark, Edie, Jerry and Kristian, who inspire and motivate me.
— L.Z.

● Printed in China. ● Library of Congress Cataloging-in-Publication Data ● Names: Swallow, Erica, author. | Zeng, Li, 1988-, illustrator. ● Title: Gabby invents the perfect hair bow / by Erica Swallow ; illustrated by Li Zeng. ● Series: Entrepreneur Kid. ● Description: Redwood City, CA: Entrepreneur Kid, 2017. ● Identifiers: ISBN 978-1-946984-01-2 (Hardcover) | 978-1-946984-10-4 (pbk.) | 978-1-946984-11-1 (ebook) | LCCN 2017939660 ● Summary: Gabby Goodwin can't stop losing her hair bows everywhere she goes. She and her mother invent a new kind of bow that doesn't fall out. ● Subjects: LCSH Goodwin, Gabby. | Young businesspeo-ple--Juvenile literature. | Businesspeople--United States--Biography--Juvenile literature. | Entrepreneurship--Ju-venile literature. | Small business--Juvenile literature. | Inventors—Juvenile literature. | Inventions--Juvenile literature. | Bows (Ribbon work)--Juvenile literature. | Mothers and daughters--Juvenile literature. ● BISAC JUVENILE NONFICTION / General | JUVENILE NONFICTION / Business & Economics | JUVENILE NONFICTION / Careers ● Classification: LCC HC102.5. G66 2017 | DDC 338.04/092--dc23 ● Printed in China ● First printing, June 2017 ● The text type was set in Capriola Regular and NTR. ● The display text was set in Sniglet and Baloo Chettan. ● The illustrations were created using Adobe Illustrator. ● Special thank you to design interns Logan Melton, Paige Yutsus, and Zhifang Wang for assistance with art.

Gabby Goodwin loves to dance. She's been taking lessons since she was three years old!

Whether she's on the stage or just heading to school, her hair is always just right.

From curls and cornrows to braids and buns, Gabby especially loves picking out colorful bows and barrettes to top off her hair styles!

"Can we do pink and red today, Mommy?" Gabby asks as she sits down for her daily hairstyling.

"You got it! Let's hope you don't lose any bows today," her mother says.

No matter where Gabby is, she always seems to lose her hair bows. As it turns out, this day would be no different.

Mrs. Goodwin dropped Gabby off for school and took her little brother to daycare before heading to work.

"Have a great day!" she told them both.

Around lunchtime, Gabby's teacher sent a photo to all of her students' parents of the kids drawing pictures in art class.

Mrs. Goodwin gasped, "Ahhh! Gabby's hair looks horrible!" Half of Gabby's barrettes were missing, and her hair was all over the place!

"Where do all of her bows go?" she thought, frantically. There had to be a way to keep the bows from falling out.

Back at home, Gabby and her little brother started their homework.

Mrs. Goodwin was frustrated as she separated the latest purchase of Gabby's hair bows by color. The family had to buy bows every two weeks, because they fell out so often.

Mrs. Goodwin picked up her phone and posted a rant online: "I can't believe it! Half of my daughter's bows are gone again! Are there any barrettes out there that actually work?"

Mothers from all around replied to Mrs. Goodwin's message.

"I can't stand those barrettes!"

 "I don't even use them anymore."

 "I twist a rubber band around them to make them stay."

 "When you find some that work, let me know."

Then, a message from the family's pastor popped up.

Pastor Bailey suggested that she make a new bow.
"Sounds like a market you need to break into," he wrote.

Mrs. Goodwin scoffed, "But I'm so busy!"

"Sounds like a market you need to break into."

Days and weeks went on. Mrs. Goodwin could not stop thinking about what the pastor had said. She wanted the problem fixed, but who was going to make these magical bows?

One morning, while styling Gabby's hair, Mrs. Goodwin huffed, "I don't even know why I'm doing your hair. Half of these bows are going to be gone when you get home."

"Mommy! Are we going to make a bow?" Gabby shouted excitedly.

"No, no, no. I was just thinking that somebody should make a bow," Mrs. Goodwin replied, placing the final barrette in Gabby's hair.

Gabby was persistent. She was five years old and loved the idea of making a new type of bow that wouldn't fall out. She asked her mom about the bow idea every day for months.

"Mommy, when will we make my bow?" she asked on the way to dance rehearsal.

"Mommy, will my bows be sold in stores?" she asked while the two were out grocery shopping.

The questions never ended.

"Mommy, wouldn't today be a great day to design a bow?" Gabby said one day.

Mrs. Goodwin couldn't say no. The two sat at the kitchen table and brainstormed.

"What do you think makes a bow stay in your hair, Gabby?" Mrs. Goodwin asked.

Gabby said they needed strong teeth. They also thought barrettes should have two faces, so people could always see the fun designs.

"Grandma hates when my bows flip the wrong way!" Gabby said.

The duo was off to work, designing the best hair barrette they could imagine!

After figuring out the type of barrette they wanted to make, they asked a friend from church to help them draw their idea, so they could share it with others. He was a really good artist and agreed to help out.

It took a few years, but Gabby's company is finally a reality.

Today, she has sold thousands of bows to kids and parents in every American state and all over the world who were tired of losing their barrettes. She's also been on national TV and radio!

Gabby and her mom make a great team. Gabby chooses bow designs and colors and names all of the products. She also handles the company's money, makes sure they have enough products, and leads sales at events.

When customers order bows online, she sends each of them a handwritten thank you card, too.

Mrs. Goodwin makes sure the business is running by partnering with other companies to manufacture and sell the bows the two designed together.

Gabby says when she grows up she wants to run her bow business with her daughter just like she and her mommy do now.

Gabby's whole family helps out with work. Her daddy is a comedian and helps her practice for speeches, since he has so much experience talking on stages. She used to get nervous, but now she can speak in front of anyone!

Even Gabby's little brother helps out — especially when Gabby throws packing parties for the days when her company gets a lot of orders. She needs tons of help when there are too many orders to handle alone!

Starting a business is hard. Not everyone wants to buy her bows. Sometimes stores don't have space to carry them either. Hearing "no" is tough, but she has learned how to deal with it.

Having school, dance, and a business makes for a busy life, too. Gabby has to miss birthday parties and playtime sometimes, so she can make sure bow orders are mailed on time. Customers are counting on her!

Gabby loves her business, though. She loves that she helps little girls keep their hair cute all day with the best hair bow ever.

These days, Gabby gives speeches all around the world, talking about her experience starting a company. Whether she's speaking to children or adults, she always encourages them to dream big.

"If you believe, you can achieve," Gabby says.
"Try your best, work hard, and never give up."

Now it's your turn... What problems do you want
to solve in the world?

Author's Note by Erica Swallow

"Gabby Invents the Perfect Hair Bow" is the story of Gabrielle "Gabby" Goodwin, who at seven years old joined forces with her mother, Rozalynn Goodwin, to invent and patent a new kind of hair barrette under the company name GaBBY Bows.

The story of GaBBY Bows begins in 2011 in Columbia, South Carolina with a social media rant from Mrs. Goodwin, who posted on social networking site Twitter that she was tired of buying faulty hair barrettes, some of which didn't even come with clasps to hold her five-year-old daughter's hair. As vividly portrayed in the book, that post resonated with parents in Mrs. Goodwin's network. Mothers near and far responded that they, too, had similar issues. Mrs. Goodwin, though, just couldn't shake a response from the Goodwin family's pastor.

"Sounds like a market you need to break into," Pastor Herbert Bailey, founder of Right Direction Church International, tweeted.

Mrs. Goodwin and husband Mike Goodwin had been attending Dr. Bailey's church since before they were parents. Dr. Bailey had seen Mike's transition from a career in college counseling to comedy, as the family-friendly "Bowtie Comedian." Dr. Bailey was also around to witness Rozalynn's expanding career in health care policy and the birth of the couple's two children, Gabby and little brother Michael. To say the least, the Goodwins had counted Dr. Bailey as a key influencer in their lives for quite some time.

So, the story continues... After months of inaction, Mrs. Goodwin accidentally voiced her frustrations over

Gabby Goodwin loses some bows at school. Photo: Andris Kinloch, A. Renee Photography

the barrettes while styling Gabby's hair. At five years old, Gabby's first response was to ask her mother if they were going to make a new bow. Though Mrs. Goodwin tried to avoid the topic at every chance, Gabby continued to ask, until one day the mother-daughter duo sat down at the kitchen table and started brainstorming.

Today, GaBBY Bows is an international brand, having launched in 2014, when Gabby was seven years old. As of the summer of 2017, GaBBY Bows products have been sold in all 50 U.S. states and 8 countries across the globe. The bows can be found online or in retailers, including Once Upon a Child. At the time of writing, GaBBY Bows offered three bow designs, inspired by names parents call their little girls: Sweet Pea, Little Lady, and Daddy's Girl. Appropriately, Daddy's Girl is designed in the shape of a bowtie, to commemorate the influence of Gabby's father in her life.

GaBBY Bows and CEO Gabby Goodwin have received many accolades in honor of their successes, including 2015 South Carolina Young Entrepreneur of the Year, 2016 SCORE and Sam's Club Small Business Champion, 2015 SBA InnovateHer Business Competition National Finalist, and 2016 SCORE Outstanding Diverse Business of the Year.

Gabby and her mother give speeches around the country to inspire other kids to dream big. While writing this book, illustrator Li Zeng, videographer Dan Ndombe, and I visited Gabby and her family. The story and pictures you've encountered in this book were all inspired by in-person and online interviews with the family. To learn more about Gabby and her company, visit entrepreneurkid.com and gabbybows.com. Both sites feature videos, photos, and more information about the making of GaBBY Bows and the Entrepreneur Kid book about the company's beginnings. For an inspirational video message from Gabby, go to gabbybows.com/pages/thanks.

Rozalynn and Gabby Goodwin with GaBBY Bows. Photo: Andris Kinloch, A. Renee Photography

The Goodwin family. Photo: Picture People

How many Entrepreneur Kid books have you read?

There are four books in the Entrepreneur Kid series. Read them all to learn how other kids like you started their own businesses. You, too, can be an Entrepreneur Kid by solving problems around you.

Go to entrepreneurkid.com to buy the full series and submit your Entrepreneur Kid story for an opportunity to be featured on our website!

Find Entrepreneur Kid on social media to share your reading experience.

@EntrepreneurKid   @EntrepreneurKid   /EntrepreneurKid   /company/EntrepreneurKid